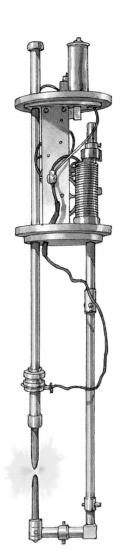

KU-649-214

CONTENTS

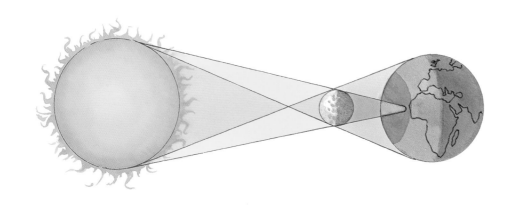

LIGHT

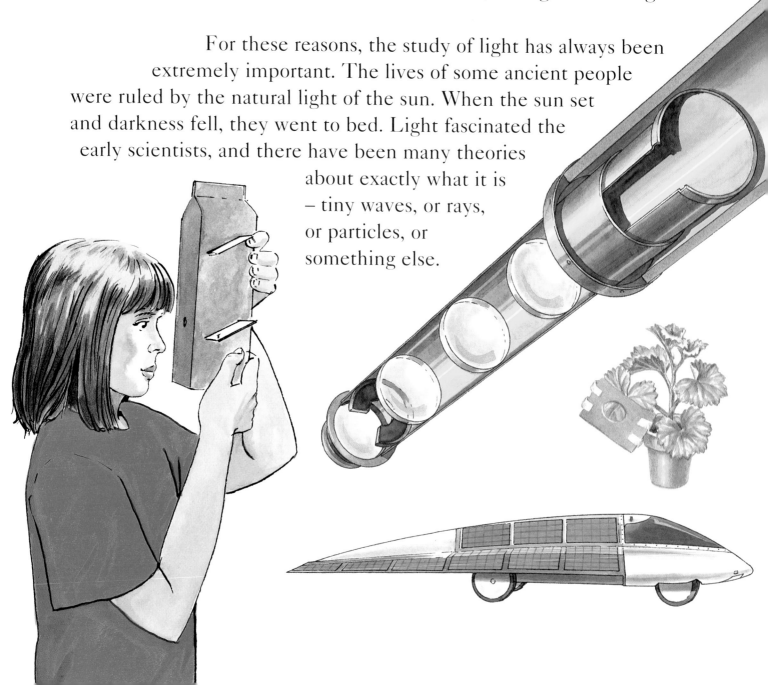

Where would we be without light? Blundering around in the dark! Humans rely mainly on sight to find out what is going on around them. Up to two-thirds of the brain's awareness is taken up by what we see, while hearing , smell and the other senses are much less important. With light to see by, we can find our food and our way, appreciate beauty, take in knowledge and watch science at work. After all, seeing is believing.

For these reasons, the study of light has always been extremely important. The lives of some ancient people were ruled by the natural light of the sun. When the sun set and darkness fell, they went to bed. Light fascinated the early scientists, and there have been many theories about exactly what it is – tiny waves, or rays, or particles, or something else.

SCIENCE WORKS!

LIGHT

STEVE PARKER

MACDONALD YOUNG BOOKS

First published in 1995 by Macdonald
Young Books Ltd

© 1995 Macdonald Young Books Ltd

Campus 400
Maylands Avenue
Hemel Hempstead
Hertfordshire
HP2 7EZ

Commissioning editor: Thomas Keegan
Designer: Jane Felstead
Editor: Chris Norris
Illustrators: Chris Lyons, Martin Woodward,
Simone End, Bob Moulder

ISBN 07500 1593 4

A CIP catalogue record for this book is available
from the British Library

Typeset by Between the Lines

Printed and bound in Hong Kong

The story of light

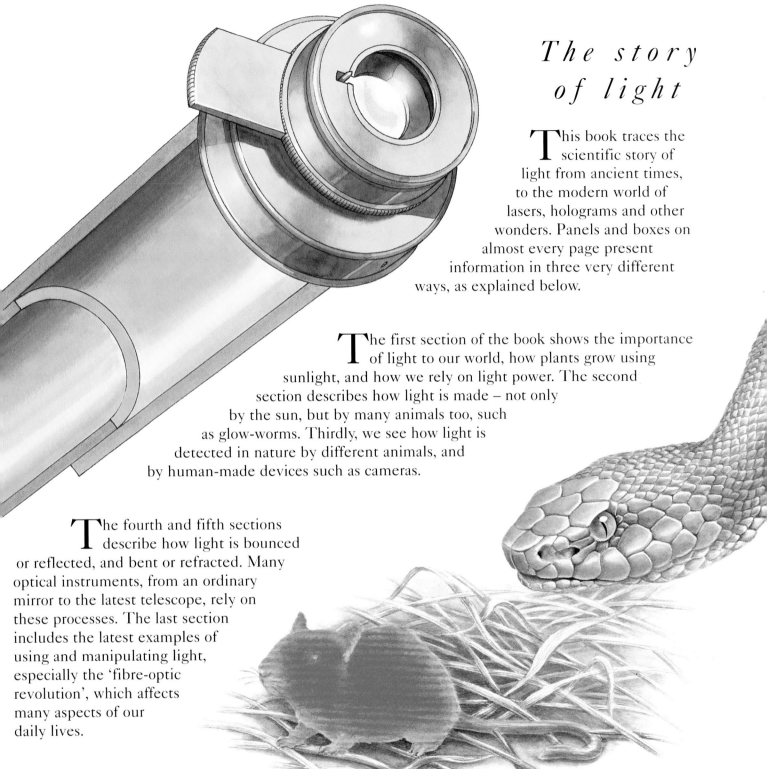

This book traces the scientific story of light from ancient times, to the modern world of lasers, holograms and other wonders. Panels and boxes on almost every page present information in three very different ways, as explained below.

The first section of the book shows the importance of light to our world, how plants grow using sunlight, and how we rely on light power. The second section describes how light is made – not only by the sun, but by many animals too, such as glow-worms. Thirdly, we see how light is detected in nature by different animals, and by human-made devices such as cameras.

The fourth and fifth sections describe how light is bounced or reflected, and bent or refracted. Many optical instruments, from an ordinary mirror to the latest telescope, rely on these processes. The last section includes the latest examples of using and manipulating light, especially the 'fibre-optic revolution', which affects many aspects of our daily lives.

FAMOUS FIRSTS

Knowledge thrives on 'firsts', such as the person to discover a scientific law or make an invention. The *Famous Firsts* panels describe who got there in front of all the others.

DIY SCIENCE

Follow in the footsteps of well-known scientists by trying the tests and experiments in Do-It-Yourself form, using everyday objects and equipment, as shown in the *DIY Science* panels.

SPECIAL FX

Scientific processes and principles can have fascinating, even startling results. The *Special FX* projects show you how to produce these special effects. Most items are easily available about the home.

NATURAL LIGHT

In the natural world light is all around. During daytime, the sun shines down and illuminates the scene. As the earth turns and the sun goes below the horizon, its light fades. But even at night, there is light – from the changing face of the moon and the twinkling stars, to the eerie glow of insects among the trees and fish in the seas.

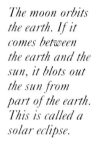

The moon orbits the earth. If it comes between the earth and the sun, it blots out the sun from part of the earth. This is called a solar eclipse.

Many people worshipped the sun as their god or chief spirit. It was seen as a fiery deity that brought light and life.

Life would not exist on earth, without light and heat from the sun. Light lets us see what we are doing and where we are going. Ancient people had no electric light bulbs, central heating or wrist-watches. They waited every day for the sun to rise and bring brightness and warmth to the world. Their clock was the path of the sun across the sky.

Ancient people also knew that the sun's light and warmth made the crops grow. In fact light is the basis of food for all creatures because of the way plants use it. Plants can trap the energy contained in light by photosynthesis (see opposite). They do this using chlorophyll, a green sub-

When the sun hid in an eclipse in ancient times, some people worried that it might never return. They prayed and offered gifts and sacrifices to the Sun God.

During an eclipse the edge of the sun shows as a halo, or corona, around the dark disc of the moon. As the moon continues its orbit, the sun is revealed again.

FASCINATING FACTS

- The sun is 1,390,000 kilometres across, which is over 100 times the earth's diameter. It is an average of 150 million kilometres from earth.

- Of the light, heat and other energy given out by the sun, only one-thousandth of one-millionth of it reaches the earth.

- Of the sun's light, heat and other energy that reaches the earth, about one-third never reaches the surface. It is reflected back into space by the atmosphere and clouds.

FAMOUS FIRSTS

THE SUNDIAL

The sundial has a central stick or pointer, the gnomon, that casts a shadow. As the sun passes across the sky, it shines from different directions. The shadow of the gnomon moves, falling on a dial that shows the time. The Babylonians first used sundials over 4000 years ago. However the sundial is no good on a cloudy day, or at night!

Sundials were often used as church clocks, which were the central point of a village.

This 16th-century double-sundial has a pointer on the upright column and one on the front face.

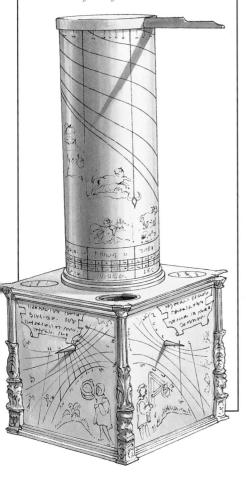

DIY SCIENCE

SUNDIAL TIME

Make a simple sundial and put it outside on a sunny day. Using a watch, mark the position of the shadow on its dial at each hour. Try the sundial a few weeks later, 'setting' it first thing in the morning. Is it still correct?

You need
Card, scissors, watch, two pencils.

1. Cut out a circle of card and push a pencil through the middle, to make the gnomon. Stick this into the ground in an unshaded place.

2. Draw and number the site of the shadow on the dial using the pencil, labelling every hour on the hour as shown by your watch.

3. A few weeks later, put the sundial in the same place. At 9 a.m. twist the dial so the gnomon's shadow falls on the 9 a.m. mark. Check the sundial later. Does the sun now have a different path? Can you think why?

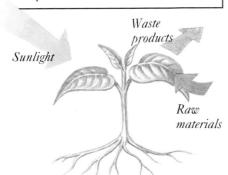

Sunlight

Waste products

Raw materials

SPECIAL FX

LIGHT FOR LIFE

Show that plants need light to live and grow. Block off light to a leaf using black paper and sticking tape. After a few days the leaf in the dark looks pale and ill, since it cannot photosynthesize to get the energy to live. Allow light to reach it again and the leaf recovers.

You need
A plant, two sheets of black paper, sticking tape.

1. Tape the sheets of paper over one of the large, strong leaves, one sheet on each side.

2. After several days, remove the paper. The leaf beneath is pale and unhealthy because of lack of light.

stance in their leaves. The chlorophyll takes in the energy and converts it into energy-rich chemicals, such as sugars in the plant's sap. The plant uses this energy to live and grow, by making its roots, stems, leaves and flowers.

Herbivorous animals eat plants, taking in the energy-rich chemicals and using them for their own living and growing processes. Carnivorous creatures eat these animals for food, getting energy and growth materials from their flesh.

In this way the original light energy from the sun passes first into plants and then into the complicated web of animal foods. The whole of life on earth is powered by light energy from the sun.

At night, ancient people would have been fascinated by the light of the stars as they seemed to whirl across the sky. They saw the shapes of humans, animals and objects in the star patterns, and invented names for them and stories about them. This was the origin of the star constellations and the signs of the zodiac. Today we tend to stay indoors at night. And we have so many lights in streets and buildings, that they blot out the natural starlight. We are largely strangers to the wonders of the night sky.

DIY SCIENCE

STRAIGHT LINES AND SHADOWS
Light shines in straight lines. It can change direction by reflection or refraction (see page 24) but, if there is nothing in the way, light travels in a straight line. If you stand in strong sunlight or near a powerful street lamp, you see your shadow on the ground. Light goes straight; it cannot bend around your body. The shadow is the place where no light reaches because it is blocked by you. The darkness of the shadow depends on how much light is coming from other sources in different directions. On a hazy day, light gets scattered by the clouds and surrounding objects, and it comes from many directions. So the shadow is more blurred and less dark, compared to the shadow in bright, clear sunlight.

Try walking nearer or farther from a street light, and see how the shadow changes in size and shape. As you walk farther from the light, do its edges become more blurred?

DIY SCIENCE

A BRIGHT SPARK
You need
Two pieces of flint rock, thick gloves, protective eye goggles, adult supervision.

You might use a match to light a fire nowadays but, before there were matches, people used rocks. The type of rock called flint produces sparks when hit. A spark is both light and heat. Pieces of flint were used in old cannons and guns, to make the sparks that lit the gunpowder. One type of gun was called the flintlock, after this use of flint.

Ensure your hands and eyes are well protected as you strike the flints together. You will notice the sparks best in dim light.

FAMOUS FIRSTS

STRAIGHT AND CURVED

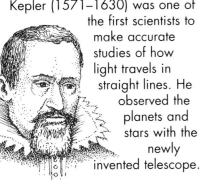

German astronomer Johannes Kepler (1571–1630) was one of the first scientists to make accurate studies of how light travels in straight lines. He observed the planets and stars with the newly invented telescope.

FASCINATING FACTS

- It is not quite true that light always goes in straight lines. If light passes near to a huge object, such as a star, it is attracted by the star's immense force of gravity. The light is bent or curved slightly nearest the star.

- In a hilly place and in misty weather conditions, light shines past you and casts a giant shadow, surrounded by coloured rings, on to mist or clouds. This is called the Brocken Spectre.

SPECIAL FX

MANY HANDS MAKE LIGHT WORK

Study shadows like scientists of the past by using candles as a light source. A candle does not cast such sharp-edged shadows as a modern torch (see below).

You need
Safety candles and matches, table, nearby white wall, adult supervision.

1. Hold your hand between the lit candle and the wall. (Keep your hands more than 30 centimetres from the candle.) Move your hand nearer the wall. Is the shadow bigger or smaller? Is it clearer or more blurred?

2. Put two lit candles side by side, and hold up your hand again. How many shadows are there? Do they overlap?

3. Carefully move one candle away from the other, and hold up your hand again. Are the shadows farther apart? Trace the light going in straight lines from each candle, past your hand to the wall.

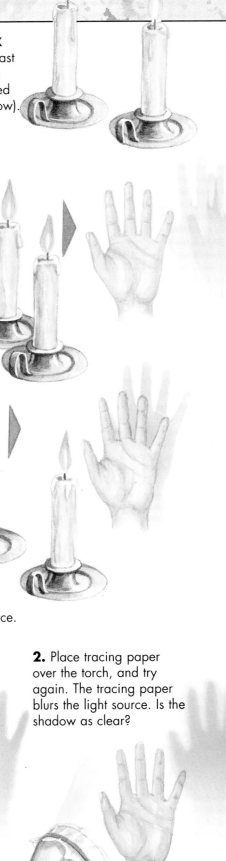

SHARP OR BLURRED?

Light from a point casts a sharper shadow than light from a larger source.

1. Using a torch with a narrow beam, shine it to cast a shadow on the wall.

2. Place tracing paper over the torch, and try again. The tracing paper blurs the light source. Is the shadow as clear?

MAKING LIGHT

The 'glow-worm' is a female beetle that makes a greenish, glowing light. She does this to attract a male partner, for breeding.

For billions of years the sun has made light by nuclear fusion. For millions of years, animals have made light by bioluminescence. For thousands of years people have seen in the dark by the light of flames. The electric light bulb was invented just over 100 years ago.

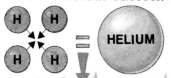

In the sun, four atoms of hydrogen join together to produce one atom of helium, giving off energy as light, heat and other forms. This is called nuclear fusion.

Our nearest star, the sun, is the main source of light for our world. It looks big and bright because it is so close to the earth. But the sun is really a fairly small star, a glowing ball of mainly hydrogen gas. It produces immense amounts of light, heat and other energy by a nuclear fusion reaction. This involves pushing together four atoms of hydrogen with incredible force, so that they join or fuse.

FAMOUS FIRSTS

LIGHT TO SEE BY
The first evidence for people using fire comes from fossil ashes at Dragon Mountain, near Beijing in China. People learned to make flaming torches from long-burning wood. Then they invented oil lamps and wax candles. These used slow-burning materials, which made a bright yellow flame. The oil soaked into a piece of rope or textile and burned slowly at its end.

This ancient Scottish oil lamp held its oil in a seashell.

The first candles were made over 5000 years ago in Crete and Egypt, using beeswax. Tallow, or solidified animal fat – especially from cattle and sheep – became a popular but smoky candle fuel.

Caves were fairly safe and sheltered, but dark. The fire gave out light and heat for warmth and cooking.

The Ancient Egyptians made portable oil lamps from clay and other pottery materials.

Surrounding the flame in a clear glass tube or cup protected it from being blown out.

DIY SCIENCE

MAKE YOUR OWN LIGHT

Make your own 'electric lamp' which gives out about the same amount of light as an oil lamp. Could you use this as your only light source, as in ancient times?

You need

A small battery (about 3 volts) with a suitable bulb and bulb-holder, two split pins, paper clip, plastic washing-up liquid bottle, sticking tape, wire.

1. Carefully cut off the top of the bottle. Keep both parts for use later.

2. Wash and dry the parts of the bottle to remove all soap and moisture.

3. Screw the bulb into the holder. Clip or screw a piece of wire to each bulb-holder contact.

4. Use sticking tape to fix the end of one wire from the bulb-holder to one battery contact.

5. Tape a third length of wire to the other battery contact. This will go to the switch.

6. Tape the battery securely into one side of the plastic bottle. Clip or screw the two free ends of wire to the switch.

7. With the scissors, carefully cut small holes for the split pins in the bottle's side. Attach the paper clip for the switch. Touch it to both pins to turn on.

8. Push the bulb into the neck of the cut-off top of the bottle, as if you were pushing it into the original, complete bottle.

9. Tape the cut-off end back on to the bottle, but the other way round. Your 'electric lamp' is now ready for use. In the evening, try it as your only light source for an hour!

FASCINATING FACTS

- The brightness of lights used to be measured in units called candles, or candlepower. The modern international standard unit is the new candle or candela.

- Most towns and cities have so many electric lights, that they outshine the stars above. Astronomers who wish to study the night sky must go to remote places, far away from city lights.

- Our sun may seem bright, but it is not especially so compared to other stars. Some giant stars produce millions of times more light (and heat). However they are so far away that they are tiny twinkling points, just like other stars.

- Shooting stars are lumps of rock from space, called meteors. They hurtle towards earth and burn up high in the atmosphere, producing a fiery trail in the night sky.

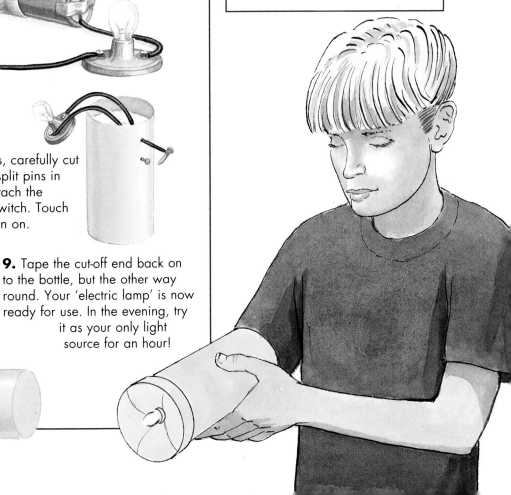

The result is one atom of the slightly heavier gas, helium, plus massive amounts of light and other energy.

Nuclear fusion happens constantly in the sun's interior, using up more than 4 million tonnes of hydrogen every second. Luckily the sun is so enormous that there is enough hydrogen to last for many millions of years into the future.

Here on earth there are many sources of light in nature. A lightning bolt is a huge spark of electrical energy that produces heat, light and sound. Some animals make light, which can be surprisingly bright. They include glow-worms and fireflies.

FAMOUS FIRSTS

Davy lamp

BRIGHT IDEAS

Explosive gases seeped through mines so that the flames of lamps often started terrible fires. Humphry Davy (1778–1829) invented a safety lamp by enclosing the flame in a wire mesh, to stop its heat reaching the gases outside. In the 19th century the first electric lamps used a continuous spark called an arc, which flickered noisily and often went out.

A spluttering arc sparked between the tips of two carbon rods. But it burned away the carbon, so the gap had to be continually adjusted.

Davy's safety lamp for miners spread out the flame's heat by a wire mesh. The dangerous gases on the outside could not get hot enough to explode.

gap

FAMOUS FIRSTS

THE COMING OF THE LIGHT BULB

After the invention of the battery in 1800, many scientists experimented with electricity. But its use was limited to special equipment in laboratories and factories. All this changed in 1879. Joseph Swan (1828–1914), in England, and famous American inventor Thomas Edison (1847–1931), separately produced the first successful light bulbs, or 'glowing lamps'. They did not use a flame or a spark. A thin filament was heated so much by electricity passing through, that it glowed white-hot. The age of electricity and cheap, powerful light had begun.

At first Swan (left) and Edison argued about who invented the light bulb first. But when they realized it would be a long, costly battle, they joined forces. Their factories were soon making millions of bulbs.

Swan's bulb *The very thin filament was mainly carbon, made from a treated piece of thread.*

Edison's bulb *As in Swan's lamp, the glass bulb had most of the air removed. With hardly any oxygen the filament could not burn away.*

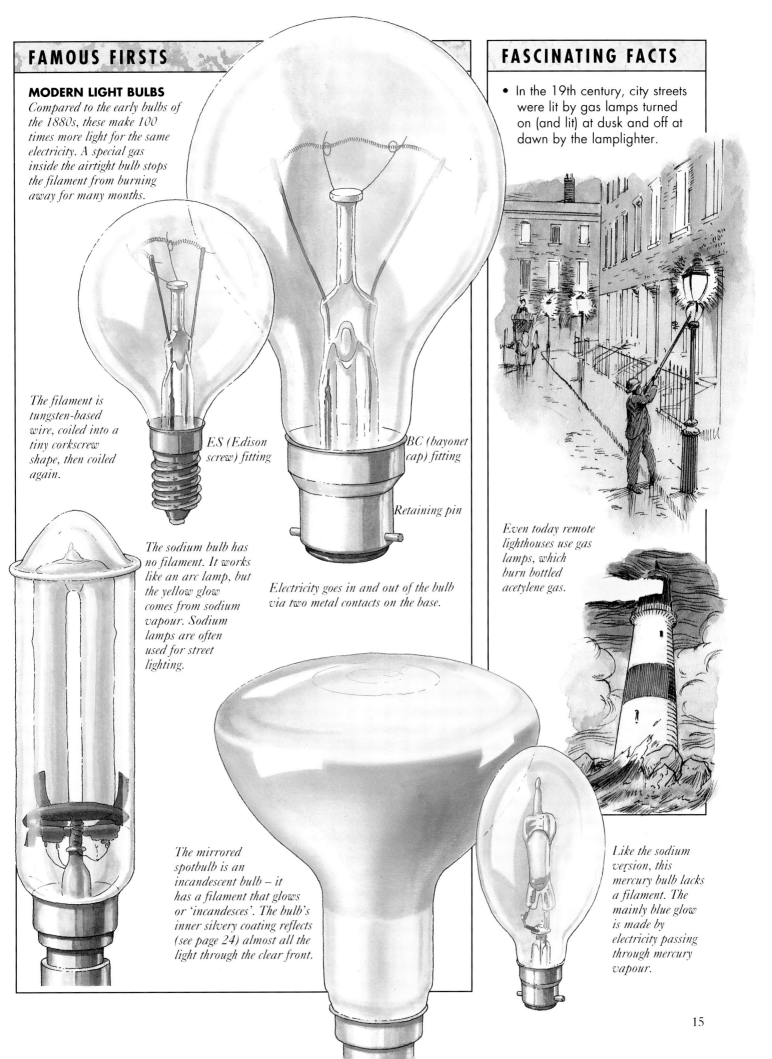

MODERN LIGHT BULBS

Compared to the early bulbs of the 1880s, these make 100 times more light for the same electricity. A special gas inside the airtight bulb stops the filament from burning away for many months.

The filament is tungsten-based wire, coiled into a tiny corkscrew shape, then coiled again.

ES (Edison screw) fitting

BC (bayonet cap) fitting

Retaining pin

The sodium bulb has no filament. It works like an arc lamp, but the yellow glow comes from sodium vapour. Sodium lamps are often used for street lighting.

Electricity goes in and out of the bulb via two metal contacts on the base.

The mirrored spotbulb is an incandescent bulb – it has a filament that glows or 'incandesces'. The bulb's inner silvery coating reflects (see page 24) almost all the light through the clear front.

- In the 19th century, city streets were lit by gas lamps turned on (and lit) at dusk and off at dawn by the lamplighter.

Even today remote lighthouses use gas lamps, which burn bottled acetylene gas.

Like the sodium version, this mercury bulb lacks a filament. The mainly blue glow is made by electricity passing through mercury vapour.

15

These are not true worms or flies, they are types of beetle. There are many light-making creatures in the sea, including jellyfish, worms, shrimps and hundreds of types of fish. In most cases of biolumines-cence, or 'living light', the glow is made when oxygen from the air combines with a substance called luciferin in the animal's skin. Most methods of making light produce heat as well, like flames and lightning. Bio-luminescence is unusual because it is 'cold light', with hardly any heat.

There have always been fires in nature, usually start-ed by lightning. But about half a million years ago our prehistoric ancestors began to 'tame' fire, for warmth, cooking, defence against wild animals – and light. Many examples have been found of stone-age camp fires, especially in caves. Some have piles of ash several metres deep, showing that the fireplace was used over many years.

The burning flame remained the main source of light for peo-ple until about a hundred years ago. Scientists had been working hard to produce light from elec-tricity, either as a continuous spark called an arc or as thin wire filament that glowed white-hot as electricity forced its way through. In 1879 two inventors succeeded with the second method. They were Thomas Edison in America and Joseph Swan in England. The light bulb was born – from that time, electric lights have lit the world.

Electrical contacts (electrodes)

Fluorescents provide bright light over large areas, as in offices and factories.

THE FLUORESCENT LIGHT
The fluorescent light is also called the strip or tube light. It does not have a filament, it works using fluorescence, as described below. French physicist Henri Becquerel made the first simple version of this lamp in 1867. But it did not come into regular use until about 1940, because of problems in manufacturing the tube, and getting it to switch on easily.

Physics pioneer Henri Becquerel (1852–1948) was interested in fluorescence and was also the first scientist to study radioactivity. He won a Nobel Prize in 1903.

HOW IT WORKS
The fluorescent lamp is a long glass tube containing a mixture of vapours, chiefly mercury (which is poisonous). A high voltage of electricity passes from one end of the tube to the other, through the vapour. The electrical energy makes the vapour 'glow', but with ultraviolet or UV light (see page 40), which we cannot see. The special phosphor coating lining the inside of the tube takes in the energy of the UV light, and changes it into visible light energy, which we see as the white glow from the tube. The process of taking in the energy of one type of light, and changing it into another type or colour of light, is called fluorescence. The flourescent light is more efficient and cheaper to run than bulbs with filaments.

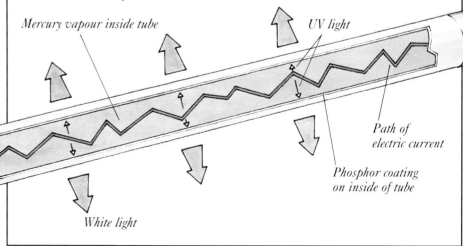

Mercury vapour inside tube

UV light

Path of electric current

Phosphor coating on inside of tube

White light

GLOW IN THE DARK

Some substances take in light energy from bright surroundings, store it for a short time, and give it out later. They can 'glow in the dark', a process called phosphorescence. (It is similar to fluorescence, see opposite, but the latter stops as soon as the incoming light ceases.) Safe phosphorescent substances are used to make toys and other items that shine in the gloom.

Road roller

Spinning top

Toy drum

Spot-glow dominoes

Glowing doll

Tin sailor

Increasing heat from sources

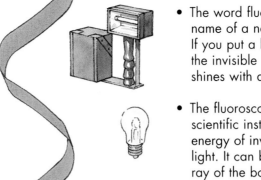

• The word fluorescence comes from the name of a natural mineral, fluorspar. If you put a lump of fluorspar under the invisible light from a UV lamp, it shines with an eerie glow.

• The fluoroscope is an important scientific instrument. It converts the energy of invisible X-rays into visible light. It can be used to view a 'live' X-ray of the body, and to examine solid substances for cracks and flaws.

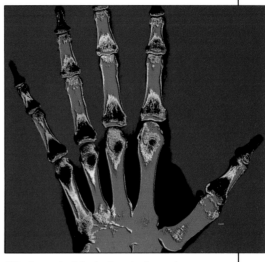

The bones inside the hand, shown by fluoroscope X-ray.

• Light rays cannot pass through the human body, but X-rays can, in controlled amounts to prevent harm. They go through soft parts easily, like blood and muscles, but not through hard parts like bones and cartilage. On an X-ray photograph, hard body bits are pale and soft parts are dark.

• The metal radium is luminescent – it gives out light. In the 1920s, 'glow in the dark' toys and watch dials used radium-containing paints. But the workers got radiation sickness, because radium is radioactive. Its use was stopped.

• Bright colours, like orange and green, are worn by cyclists and others who need to be seen. These are sometimes called 'luminous' or 'flourescent', but they are just highly reflective. They reflect most light that falls on them, adding their own colour as they do so.

DETECTING LIGHT

We detect light with our eyes as part of our daily lives. We also have machines to record and measure light energy, such as cameras and light meters (see pages 22 and 28). Light energy can be changed or converted into others forms of energy, such as energy-rich chemicals, heat or electricity.

Some insects see light which our own eyes cannot quite detect. A bee sees ultraviolet light (see page 40), showing up as patterns on flower petals.

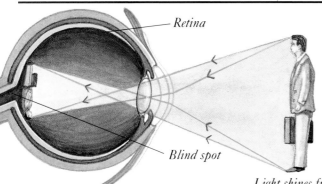

Retina

Blind spot

Light shines from objects into the eye. It is detected as chemical changes in the retina and then turned into electrical nerve signals.

In order to study and use light, you must be able to detect it. You are doing this now, using the most familiar of light-detectors – your eyes. Light is defined as 'light' because it is the type of energy which is detected by human eyes.

The eyes detect light by a two-stage process. First, light shines into your eye and on to the retina, a very thin layer inside the eyeball. Here the energy of each tiny patch of light causes chemical changes in substances known as visual pigments.

Second, the chemical changes in the visual pigments trigger tiny bursts of electricity, which form nerve signals. These flash along nerves to your brain. It happens at incredible speed. Every second in the retina, millions of visual pigments detect millions

Clams and scallops have tiny jewel-like eyes. But these do not see clearly. They only pick up patches of light or dark.

DIY SCIENCE

THROUGH FLY'S EYES
An insect like a fly has an eye with hundreds of separate parts. Each sees a small patch of the scene, as shown by this experiment.

You need
A pencil, card, tracing paper, sticking tape, newspaper.

1. Carefully cut a small hole in the card sheet. Tape the tracing paper over a photo in the newspaper. Put the card over this. Look through the hole at the tiny patch of photo. Is it light or dark?

2. With the pencil, shade the tracing paper through the hole, light or dark as you see it. Repeat 100 times, moving the hole to different parts of the photo. Lift the tracing paper to see a mosaic-type set of shaded dots, like a fly's eye view.

SPECIAL FX

TRICKS WITH LIGHT

We can make sense of most natural patterns of light detected by our eyes. We can also make 'artificial' scenes called visual or optical illusions, that look puzzling or even impossible. However, these illusions do not trick the eye. The eye simply detects the colours and patterns of light reaching it and passes nerve signals to the brain. Visual illusions trick the brain as to how it interprets and makes sense of the signals.

HOW TO FIND YOUR BLIND SPOT

You need
Card, dark crayon

1. Crayon two dots on to the card, 10 cms apart, then hold it about 30 cms from your face. Close one eye. Look at one of the dots with the other eye. Slowly bring the page nearer, still looking at the first dot.

2. When the light rays from the second dot falls on your eye's blind spot, the dot disappears. Now look over towards the second dot. The light rays fall on a normal part of your eye's retina. The dot reappears as if by magic!

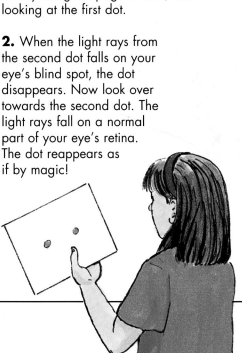

This ball could be covered with raised lumps or small pits. Your brain assumes light comes from above, which it usually does. The shadows cast downwards suggest pits, while upwards they suggest lumps.

Which is longer? *Guess which straight, central line is longer by looking only. Then measure their lengths with a ruler.*

Which is bigger?
The cats in this 'room' look different sizes, with the one on the left being the smallest. But they are all the same size. The effect is due to the lines which make the cats appear to be different distances away.

The eternal triangle is a flat drawing that uses shading to make it look solid. The picture below, makes good sense. But drawn with all three sides joined (below right) it seems to go on for ever.

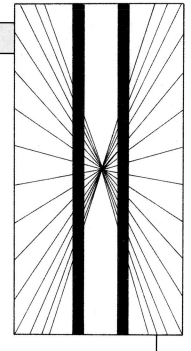

Which is straighter?
The many lines coming from a central point, like wheel spokes, make the two vertical lines appear curved. Use a ruler to check if they are.

Your eyes each have a tiny area of retina called the blind spot, which sees nothing. Each eye fills in the missing detail for the other. Close one eye, and the blind spot is revealed. How can the magician make the frog disappear? Hint: it's like the dots on the card on the far left of this page.

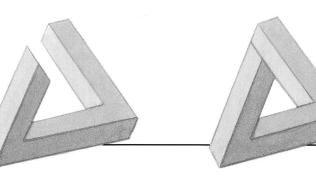

of tiny patches of light. Incredible numbers of nerve signals flash to the brain. The brain analyses them to build up a picture of the world you see, showing shapes, patterns and movements in full colour.

We can remember what our eyes see, but memories fade. An artist can draw or paint a scene, but this is a personal view which is never completely exact. People wanted to invent a device that would detect light accurately and make a permanent record of it.

The result was photography, or 'writing with light'. The photographic camera uses the same principle as the eye. The energy in light causes changes in a layer of silver-based chemicals, which we call a film. This produces a copy, or photograph, of the pattern of light. The first photographs were taken in the 1820s.

Soon people wanted to record more than single, still photographs. They wanted movement, just as in real life.

FAMOUS FIRSTS

PIONEERS OF PHOTOGRAPHY

In 1727 scientists noticed that certain silver-containing chemicals turned dark when exposed to light. However it took 100 years for Joseph Niepce to use this effect to make the first true photograph. Another 70 years passed before photography developed into a practical process, cheap and easy enough for almost anyone to use.

Joseph Niepce (1765–1833)

Early photographs needed lots of light. So the subjects had to sit very still for many minutes.

William Fox Talbot (1800–77) invented the negative photograph, with dark areas showing up lightest. Many positive prints could be made from one negative. He called these calotypes.

Calotype camera

Daguerre cameras had a sliding rear portion. This was moved in or out to make the picture focus on the plate.

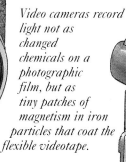

Like most cameras, Fox Talbot's used a lens to focus a clear, sharp picture (see page 32).

Video cameras record light not as changed chemicals on a photographic film, but as tiny patches of magnetism in iron particles that coat the flexible videotape.

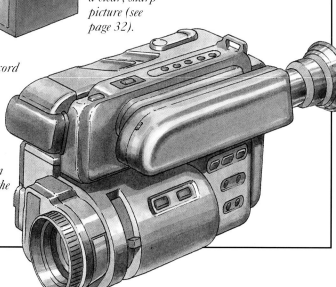

Today's camera fits into a pocket. It automatically measures the light level, focuses on a scene and winds on the film.

DIY SCIENCE

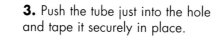

SEE-THROUGH CAMERA
Most cameras have a lens to focus the light rays.

You need
Cardboard box and tube, tracing paper, sticking tape, large magnifying lens.

1. Place the tube on one side of the box, and draw a circle around it.

2. Carefully cut around the circle to make a hole. Cut out the whole side of the box opposite the hole.

3. Push the tube just into the hole and tape it securely in place.

4. Tape the tracing paper on to the box, in place of the missing side opposite the tube.

5. Hold the magnifying lens over the open end of the tube, in the position shown.

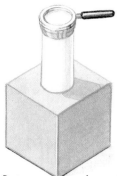

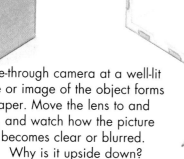

6. Point your see-through camera at a well-lit object. A picture or image of the object forms on the tracing paper. Move the lens to and fro, and watch how the picture becomes clear or blurred. Why is it upside down?

FASCINATING FACTS

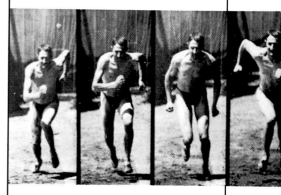

- Eadweard Muybridge (1830–1904) was a pioneer of fast-action photography for movement, where each picture is taken a very short time after the previous one. In 1877 he photographed a running horse using a bank of 24 cameras worked by trip wires. This settled a wager that the horse had all four feet off the ground for a split second – it did. Muybridge also photographed people and other animals in motion.

- Today's fast-action cameras take thousands of pictures each second. They can 'freeze' movements too fast for our eyes to see, such as the beating of an insect's wings.

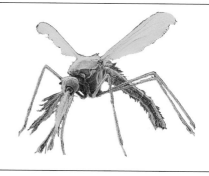

- Colour photography lagged behind black-and-white photography. It took much research to find the right mixture of chemicals, each responding to a different colour and brightness of light. It did not become practical until the early 1900s for stills and the 1950s for movies.

Inventors soon devised machines to take, and then show, many still photographs in a fast sequence of about 25 per second. The eye cannot distinguish between them, and the photos blur into each other to create continuous movement. The movie camera, and the projection system for shining the pictures on to a screen, were developed in the 1890s.

Then scientists began to work on the idea of not only detecting light, but using its energy to do useful work. However light's energy is relatively weak compared to many other energy forms. Using light energy had to wait until the development of sensitive electronic circuits during the 1950s and 1960s.

Movie cameras use large rolls of photographic film wound on to two spools in a case above the camera body. The tripod keeps the camera steady so the images are not blurred, yet it lets the camera swing sideways or 'pan'.

FASCINATING FACTS

THE FIRST MOVIES

During the late 1800s inventors worked feverishly to make the first movies or cinema films. The system needed many photographs taken in fast succession (see opposite). This became possible with celluloid film on a flexible strip, invented in 1887 by American George Eastman. In the 1890s Thomas Edison's kinetoscope played back short movies in a 'peep-show' box for one viewer at a time.

Cinema truly arrived in 1895 with the first movie film by the Lumière brothers, projected on to a screen in Paris for many viewers.

Louis Lumière (1864–1948) and his brother Auguste (1862–1954) invented a device called the cinématographe. It was a camera to take the photographs and also a projector to shine them in fast succession on the screen.

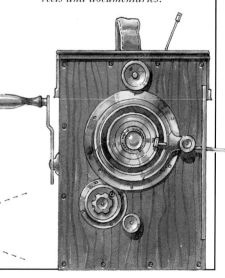

The mutascope worked like a flicker-book, showing many photograph prints in quick succession for one viewer at a time.

Movie cameras became more reliable and portable. They recorded feature films, news reels and documentaries.

Inside a movie camera, the strip of film winds off one reel, goes past the rear of the lens, and winds onto a take-up spool.

SPECIAL FX

MOVING PICTURES

Zoetropes showed still pictures in quick succession like a movie film.

You need

Card, sticking tape, pencil.

1. Carefully cut a long card strip. Draw about 20 lines to mark it into squares. Draw a stick figure that moves slightly, from one square or 'frame' to the next.

2. Tape the card strip to a card disc, like a wheel, with the pictures on the outside. Push the pencil through the middle of the disc and tape it in place.

3. Carefully cut a small hole in another sheet of card, and look through this. Spin the wheel fast like a top, on a smooth table. See how the pictures whizz past and blur into each other. You can make a flicker-book that creates the same effect.

FAMOUS FIRSTS

LIGHT POWER

Light is changed into electricity using photoelectric cells, first developed in the 1920s. A photoelectric cell powered by sunlight is called a solar cell. An average cell produces about 0.6-1.0 volts. Many cells connected together produce higher voltages. One drawback is that they only make useful amounts of electricity in very bright light.

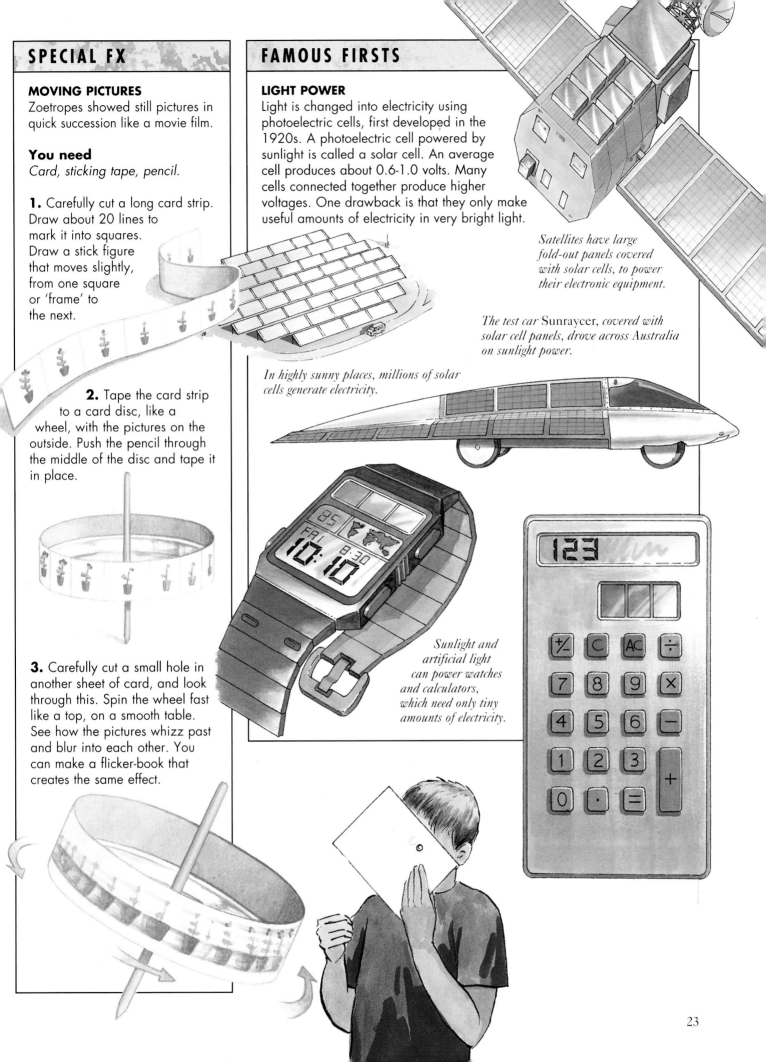

Satellites have large fold-out panels covered with solar cells, to power their electronic equipment.

The test car Sunraycer, *covered with solar cell panels, drove across Australia on sunlight power.*

In highly sunny places, millions of solar cells generate electricity.

Sunlight and artificial light can power watches and calculators, which need only tiny amounts of electricity.

BOUNCING LIGHT

L ong ago, people looked into a still pool of water – and realized that they could see their own faces. This happens by the process of light from an object bouncing off a smooth surface, and entering our eyes. We call it reflection. We have hundreds of uses for reflection today, from the bathroom mirror to the latest cameras and optical fibres.

Light from the sun reflects of your friend and then into your eyes.

Light bounces off most objects. This is how we see them. The light from the sun or another source bounces from their surfaces, and enters your eyes.

However, most surfaces are rough and not shiny. So the light bounces off them in a random way. But a very smooth, shiny surface allows light to bounce off it very precisely, with the same pattern that it had before it arrived at the surface. This arriving light pattern represents a picture or image of whatever it had bounced off before. So a smooth, shiny surface such as a mirror simply passes on, or reflects, the image of the previous object straight to your eyes.

A simple example is looking in a mirror. Light from the sun or other source bounces off your face. Some of this light reaches the mirror. It has a pattern of colours and brightnesses that represents what your face looks like. This light reflects from the mirror's silver-smooth surface in a very precise, accurate way, keeping its pattern. Then it enters your eyes, still carrying

Look at a friend on a pond bank. You see light coming directly, and also light reflecting from the water's surface, which forms an upside-down image.

SPECIAL FX

MIRROR-WRITING
Can you do mirror-writing? This is writing that is back to front, so when you see its image in a mirror, it looks normal. The brilliant Italian scientist and artist Leonardo da Vinci made many of his notes in mirror-writing.

Leonardo da Vinci (1452–1519)

Can you write like this? Neatly?

How well can you read backwards without using a mirror?

FAMOUS FIRSTS

A TREASURED BOOK
The Egyptian physicist Alhazen (965–1038) studied flat and curved mirrors, as well as lenses and the eye. His book *The Treasury of Optics* also discussed ideas about colours and pinhole cameras. Alhazen was one of the first scientists to work out the law of reflection, shown opposite.

Unlike many of his fellow scientists, he believed that light went from objects around into the eye, rather than coming out of the eye on to objects. Alhazen also studied irrigation schemes for the River Nile, and pretended he was mad for many years to avoid his King's displeasure.

THE LAW OF REFLECTION

Look from here

You need
Torch, sheets of card, mirror, protractor, pencil, dark place to experiment.

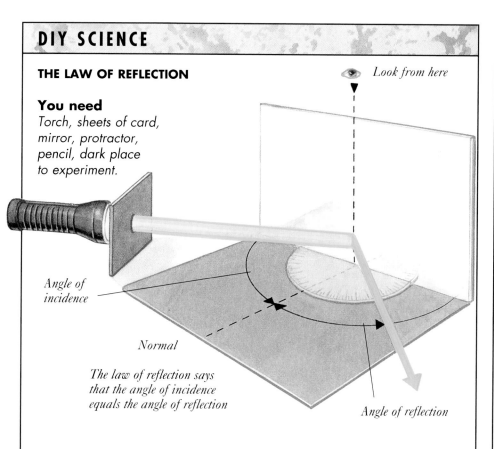

Angle of incidence

Normal

The law of reflection says that the angle of incidence equals the angle of reflection

Angle of reflection

1. Cut a small hole in one sheet of card. Arrange this card, a torch, a mirror and a flat sheet of card as shown above. Place the protractor at the point where the narrow torch beam reflects off the mirror.

2. Draw a line at 90° to the mirror, called the normal. For different torch positions, measure the angle between the torch beam and the normal, and the reflected beam and the normal. They should be equal.

FASCINATING FACTS

The first mirrors were simply bowls of water. Then polished metals, such as bronze, were used by the Ancient Egyptians.

A shaving mirror gives an enlarged or magnified view.

CURVED MIRRORS
The shiny surface of a new spoon acts as a curved mirror. Look at each side in turn. Can you see how the images differ? On the inner or concave side, you may see a tiny upside-down image of your face. On the bulging or convex side, you see a wide-angle upright view called a virtual image.

Concave mirror

Convex mirror

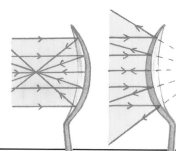

Concave mirror
The light rays come together in front of the spoon at a point called the focus. Here they cross over and spread out.

Convex mirror
The light rays reflect outwards, and appear to come from behind the spoon.

the pattern of colours and brightnesses that it had when it left your face. So you see a picture of your own face, which is known as a reflection or mirror-image.

Many scientists of ancient time thought that light was produced in the eye. It came out and shone onto the surroundings, making pictures of objects in the same way as a movie projector shines pictures onto a screen. In the 11th century, the Egyptian scientist Alhazen (see page 24) thought that light might travel in the opposite direction, from objects into the eye. His work laid part of the foundations for optics – the science and study of light.

The Ancient Greeks and Romans had some understanding of the basic science behind reflection. They certainly took advantage of the process, too. They used dark-coloured bowls of water as mirrors. They also made mirrors from flat sheets of highly polished metal such as bronze. When glass and silvered mirrors became available, in the 14th century, people could see much clearer, sharper images in their 'looking glasses'.

Gradually these more effective mirrors found their way into everyday life. People invented devices such as the periscope, which uses reflections from two mirrors to see over the top or around the side an object. Periscopes were first used widely in the trench warfare of the 19th century. In the optical toy called the kaleidoscope, the reflection of objects in one mirror is itself reflected in another mirror. The kaleido-

THE COLOURFUL KALEIDOSCOPE

You will need
Sheets of card, scissors, tracing paper, pencil, sticky tape, two small plastic-edged mirrors, coloured beads, torch.

1. Fold or tape a sheet of card into a triangular tube. Each side should be about the same size as one of the mirrors.

2. Place the tube on another card sheet, draw around it, and carefully cut out the shape.

3. Carefully cut a small viewing hole in this piece, about 2-3 centimetres across.

4. Tape the mirrors inside the tube, on two sides, before taping the end into place.

5. Follow steps 2-4 but use tracing paper, and do not cut a viewing hole in it.

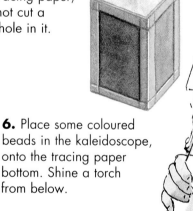

6. Place some coloured beads in the kaleidoscope, onto the tracing paper bottom. Shine a torch from below.

FASCINATING FACTS

GHOSTS ON STAGE
The Pepper's ghost uses a large, upright glass sheet on a theatre stage. The glass works as both window and mirror. The audience can see things behind it, and also reflections of things at the side of the stage. With careful lighting, a person at the side looks like a 'ghost' and seems to walk through objects on the stage.

SEEING AROUND CORNERS

You need
Tall box or carton, pencil, scissors, card sheets, two small plastic-edged mirrors, adult supervision

1. Using a triangle of card, draw a line on the top part of the box side. Make sure it is at exactly 45° to the long, upright side of the box. Draw a line sloping the same way on the lower part of the box.

2. Carefully cut a slit along the lower line, which should be just large enough to push the mirror through. Cut a slit in the upper line too.

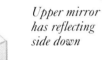

3. Draw and cut slits on the opposite side of the box, sloping the opposite way.

Upper mirror has reflecting side down

4. Push one of the small mirrors through each pair of slits, as shown, to check that it fits. Adjust the slits as necessary to give a firm fit.

Lower mirror has reflecting side up

5. Carefully cut a viewing window in front of the upper mirror, so you can see its reflecting side. Cut another viewing window behind the lower mirror, again so you can see its reflective surface.

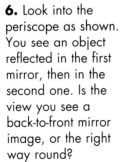

6. Look into the periscope as shown. You see an object reflected in the first mirror, then in the second one. Is the view you see a back-to-front mirror image, or the right way round?

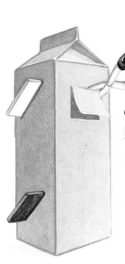

- Rigid periscope-type devices called endoscopes were used for looking into the body to check for illness and disease. The modern flexible versions use fibre optics (see page 45).

- Very complicated and delicate periscopes over 10 metres long are used on submarines. Only the top of the periscope sticks out of the water, while the submarine stays out of sight below.

The submarine periscope shows a view at the surface.

scope was invented by Scottish physicist David Brewster (1781–1868), who specialized in the reflection and polarization of light (see page 29). He also improved the design of lighthouses.

Some substances do not reflect light – they let is pass through. If some of the light gets through but it is mixed and scattered, you can see the light and vague shapes on the other side, but you cannot see a clear view. The substance is called translucent. If the light passes through without scattering and you can see a clear view, the substance is called transparent.

One of the most useful transparent substances is glass. It was invented in Ancient Egypt, and came into common use during Roman times for bowls, goblets and other containers, and decorative beads and ornaments. Glass for windows was not needed in warm countries. Glazed (glassed) windows became more common in northern Europe during medieval times, to keep wind and rain out but let the light through. A house with glazed windows was the sign of a very rich owner.

Coloured glass is made by adding certain substances during the glass-making process, such as chromium for green, copper or selenium for red, and cobalt or copper for blue. Pieces of coloured glass were used to make the much-prized 'stained-glass' windows in churches. Today, transparent plastics such as perspex and acrylic have taken over some of glass's uses. They are much lighter and do not shatter, but they are also softer and scratch more easily.

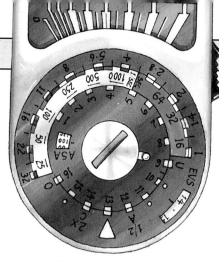

DIY SCIENCE

WHICH TORCH IS BRIGHTEST?

You need
Selection of torches, sheets of translucent paper such as tracing paper.

1. This simple light meter checks which torch is brightest. In the same dim conditions for each torch, put sheets of translucent paper over each torch until you can no longer see the light shining through. The torch which needs the most sheets is brightest!

Real light meters use sensitive electronic circuits to measure how much light energy changes to electrical energy.

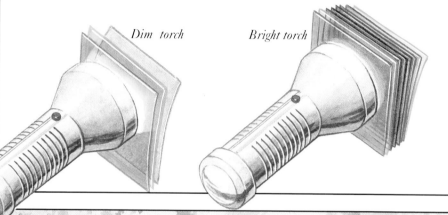

Dim torch   *Bright torch*

SPECIAL FX

LIGHT UP A SCENE

You need
Scissors, card, sticking tape, different coloured sheets of transparent plastic or cellophane (such as sweet wrappers)

1. Make a stained-glass window like those in churches. Draw a scene on the card – even a prehistoric one!

2. Carefully cut the transparent pieces to fit the scene, choosing different colours. Tape them together over the card, then cut away the inside of the card to leave a frame for your 'stained-glass window' scene.

Hold a torch behind the window, to make the colours show up more brightly.

DIY SCIENCE

REFLECTING TWISTED LIGHT: THE LCD

You can think of light as waves undulating in all directions (see page 40). When all the waves undulate in the same direction, this known as polarized light. An LCD (Liquid Crystal Display), as on a calculator, does not give out light. It uses polarization and reflection.

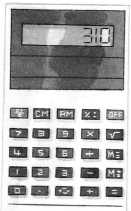

Polarized light

Normal light *Screen*

The polarizing screen is like a grid. It lets through only waves undulating in a certain direction.

The front screen polarizes the light waves. The 'off' crystal twists them. The waves go through a second screen, reflect from the back, and follow the reverse path out. The reflection makes the area look light.

The 'on' parts of the crystal no longer twist the polarized light waves at right angles. So they cannot go through the second screen, and there is no reflection. These parts of the crystal therefore look dark.

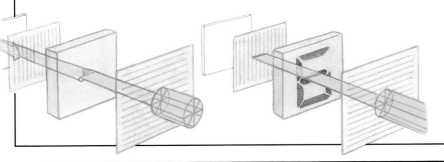

FASCINATING FACTS

- When light reflects from certain surfaces, such as water, it is partly polarized. Polaroid sunglasses (right) can help to filter out the unwanted light waves and reduce shiny glare from reflections.

- Polarized sunglasses can help pilots, drivers, skiers, sailors and other people who may be troubled by shiny surfaces, reflections and glare.

- Bees detect light that we cannot, such as ultraviolet light (see page 40). They can also see the direction of polarization in light. Clouds polarize light from the sun. So even on cloudy days, bees know the position of the sun, from its polarized light.

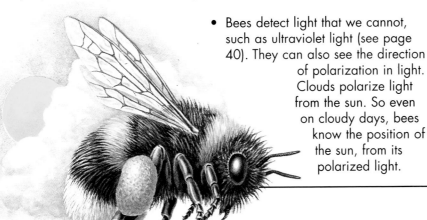

SPECIAL FX

SHADES TO BLACK

You need
Two pairs of polaroid (polarizing) sunglasses.

1. Hold the two pairs of sunglasses at the same angle so that one lens is behind the other, as shown. Look through and note the darkness of the view.

2. Turn one pair, keeping the other steady. The view slowly darkens. The rear pair polarize the light waves. As the other pair twist to right angles, none of the waves can get through its lens.

No light gets through polaroid lenses at right angles.

BENDING LIGHT

I f you see a valuable coin on the bottom of the swimming-pool, and you want to swim down and get it, beware! At a quick glance, the pool may seem shallow. But light does not always travel in straight lines. It bends when it goes from one substance, such as water, to another, such as air. The pool is always deeper than it looks.

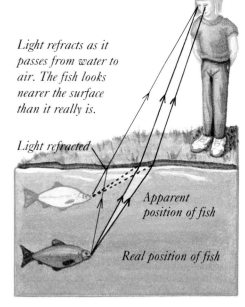

Light refracts as it passes from water to air. The fish looks nearer the surface than it really is.

Light refracted

Apparent position of fish

Real position of fish

The bending of light when it goes from one substance to another is called refraction. It happens because the speed of light (see page 42) changes as it passes across the boundary, or interface, between different substances. This happens, for example, when light goes from air, into glass or water – and when it comes back out into the air.

Ancient people probably knew about refraction. Perhaps they tried to hunt fish by standing on the bank and hurling a spear into the water. However they would soon realize that, even though the aim seemed accurate, the spear always missed the fish. Some simple experiments would show that aiming the spear below the fish would be more successful. This is because the light from the fish bends, or refracts, towards the horizontal as it leaves the water and travels to the eyes. The brain guesses that the light is travelling in straight lines. So it follows the line of sight into the water and sees an image of the fish in a certain

FAMOUS FIRSTS

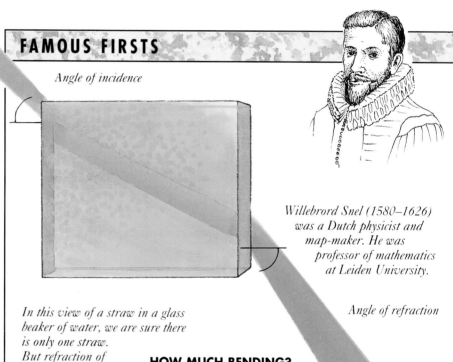

Angle of incidence

Willebrord Snel (1580–1626) was a Dutch physicist and map-maker. He was professor of mathematics at Leiden University.

Angle of refraction

In this view of a straw in a glass beaker of water, we are sure there is only one straw. But refraction of light by the glass and water make it appear like two or three.

HOW MUCH BENDING?

Ancient Egyptians such as Alhazen (see page 24) studied refraction, but could not predict it precisely. The scientific law describing the exact amount of refraction was found in 1621, by Willebrord Snel. The angle of the light before refraction and the angle after refraction have a mathematical relationship, depending on the substances concerned (see opposite). These angles are measured between the beam of light and the normal (a line at right angles to the surface); as for the angles of incidence and reflection (see page 25). The 'refracting power' of a substance – how much it bends light – is called its refractive index.

DIY SCIENCE

THE POWER OF REFRACTION

You can recreate some of Snel's experiments on refraction, using everyday items. For this version, you will need a transparent tray such as a food packaging plastic tray. It must have upright sides, not sloping sides. You are comparing the refracting power of various liquids.

You need

Torch, card with slit, large sheet of paper or card, pencil, protractor, transparent tray, transparent liquids such as water, cooking oil.

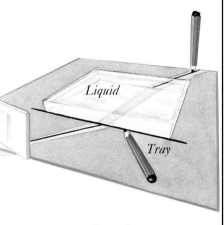

Light beam from torch

Liquid

Tray

1. Arrange the torch, slit card, tray, and large paper sheet as shown. Put the first test liquid into the tray, 5-7 centimetres deep. In dark conditions, shine the torch beam through the slit at the tray.

2. With the protractor, measure the angles of incidence and refraction, as shown in the diagram on the right. Try another test liquid, with the torch beam at the same angle of incidence. Is the angle of refraction the same?

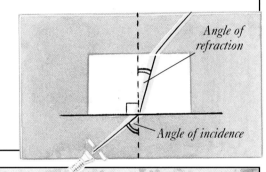

Normal

Angle of refraction

Angle of incidence

FASCINATING FACTS

- Sometimes light is refracted as it passes from air at a certain temperature into warmer or cooler air. This is the basis of a mirage. You see an image of an object which is not really in that position.

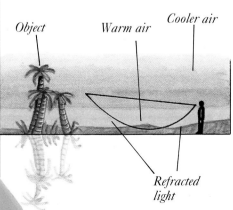

Object   *Warm air*   *Cooler air*

Refracted light

Mirage or image, where object appears to be

Mirages happen at sea as well as in the desert. In this photograph, the real island is at the top. Its reflection on the boundary between warm and cool air, just above the sea's surface, is below.

SPECIAL FX

If light arrives at a boundary, for example between air and water, it may not be refracted into the water. It may be reflected back into the air, as if from a mirror. The angle of incidence must be large for this to happen. It is called total internal reflection, and is the basis of fibre-optics (see page 45).

REFRACTION TO REFLECTION

You need

Torch, clear tank of water, white card.

1. Shine the torch at right angles to the side of the tank. The angle of incidence is zero. The beam passes straight through, with no refraction.

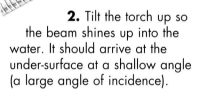

2. Tilt the torch up so the beam shines up into the water. It should arrive at the under-surface at a shallow angle (a large angle of incidence).

3. The beam should reflect from the under-surface, like a mirror, rather than passing through into the air. What is the critical angle at which this happens?

place. But the real position of the fish is slightly lower.

Refraction can also happen in air, between layers of air at different temperatures. This is the basis of the mysterious image called the mirage (see page 31), often seen in deserts or above hot, dark tarmac roads. The refraction of light as it passes through air layers in this way is taken into account when aiming guns and missiles long distances. The target is not actually where it appears to be!

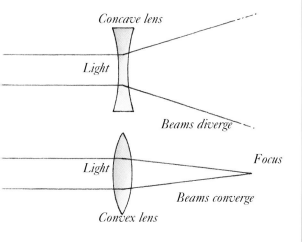

Concave lens

Light

Beams diverge

Light

Focus

Beams converge

Convex lens

There are two basic lens shapes. A convex lens is bulging and makes light beams come together, or converge, to a point called the focus. A concave lens is curved inwards and makes light beams spread out, or diverge. These lenses can correct sight problems caused by the eye's own lens or the eyeball's size. In short sight, for example, the eye's lens is too strong, or the eyeball is too big, and the images come to a focus in front of the retina

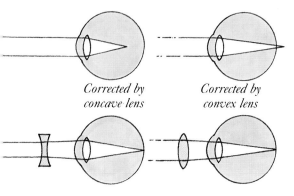

Short sight
Eye lens too strong

Long sight
Eye lens too weak

Corrected by concave lens

Corrected by convex lens

SEEING STARS
A shaving mirror has a gentle bulge or outward curve like a convex lens. This produces the effect of magnifying the image you see in it, rather like the underside of a spoon (see page 25). You can use this magnification to get a closer look at the moon and stars.

You will need
Shaving mirror, magnifying lens, flat mirror.

1. On a moonlit night, arrange the shaving mirror near a window so it reflects the moon into the flat mirror, as shown. Look at the reflection in the flat mirror through the magnifying lens.

2. The shaving mirror is curved so that it magnifies the image. This enlarged image is made even bigger by the magnifying lens. **Warning:** never do this by day. Looking at sunlight can harm your eyes.

Moon

Flat mirror

Magnifying lens

Shaving mirror

SEEING INTO OUTER SPACE
The telescope has two (or more) lenses and makes faraway objects appear much closer. It was probably invented in Holland in about 1608. The first famous telescope-user was Galileo, who studied our own Moon, and the nearby planets and their moons.

Galileo Galilei (1564–1642) used telescopes from about 1609. He described mountains on the Moon and moons around the planet Jupiter, in his book Sidereal Messenger *(1610).*

This is a replica of one of Galileo's early telescopes. It magnified (made things appear bigger) by about 30 times.

Secondary lenses

Eyepiece lens

REFRACTING TELESCOPE

This works by refraction, using lenses. It usually has a large convex lens at the front, called the objective lens, and a smaller convex lens nearer the eye, known as the eyepiece lens. The principle is shown in the diagram below using one lens.

The smaller tube slides along inside the larger one. This alters the distance between the lenses, for focusing the telescope – adjusting it for a clear, sharp view, depending on the distance of the object.

Objective lens

REFLECTING TELESCOPE

This works by reflection, using a bowl-shaped or concave mirror. The first one was designed by the famous English scientist Isaac Newton in the 1660s.

A model of Isaac Newton's first reflecting telescope.

The observer looks into the side of the telescope at the smaller secondary mirror. The advantage of mirrors is that they do not split light into its colours as much as lenses do (see page 36). So the reflecting telescope gives a clearer, sharper image.

FASCINATING FACTS

- The largest refracting telescope in the world is at the Yerkes Observatory in Wisconsin, USA. Its main lens is 101 centimetres across.

- The largest reflecting telescope is at the Keck Observatory on Mauna Kea in Hawaii, USA. Its main mirror is 10 metres across, made of 36 separate segments.

Mount Palomar. This is the largest single-mirror reflecting telescope, in California, USA. The mirror is 508 centimetres across.

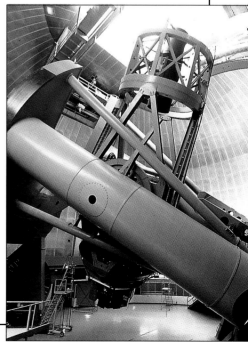

You can see a simple example of refraction by putting a pencil half into a glass of water. The lower part of the pencil looks bent at an angle, compared to the upper part. The bend is at the place where the pencil meets the surface of the water. Of course, common sense tells us that the pencil is not really bent. It is an optical illusion – a trick of the light that fools our eyes and brain (see page 30). This particular illusion is so common that we get used to it, and do not notice it as anything remarkable.

Refraction is put to use in all manner of devices and equipment, in the form of lenses. A lens is a piece of transparent substance such as glass or plastic, that has a curved shape. Light is refracted in a certain way as it passes through a lens, according to the lens' shape. Spectacle makers are constantly trying to produce new clear glasses and plastics with higher indexes of refraction than before. This enables them to make spectacle and contact lenses which are thinner, lighter and less obvious on the wearer.

Lenses can correct eyesight problems caused by the incorrect shape of the eye's own lens. They can make things seem nearer in telescopes, and make things look bigger in microscopes. Many advances in the understanding of refraction and lenses happened in the 1600s, with the invention of the telescope and microscope, and the discovery of the law of refraction by Willebrord Snel (see page 30).

FAMOUS FIRSTS

SEEING INTO INNER SPACE

A microscope, like a telescope, makes things appear larger. It also has one or more lenses. The curvature of the lenses and the distance between them is adjusted to look at very tiny objects, rather than very distant ones as in the telescope. The microscope was probably invented in the 1590s by Dutch craftsman Zacharias Janssen.

In his spare time, Dutch draper Antoni van Leeuwenhoek (1632–1723) made his own single-lens microscopes.

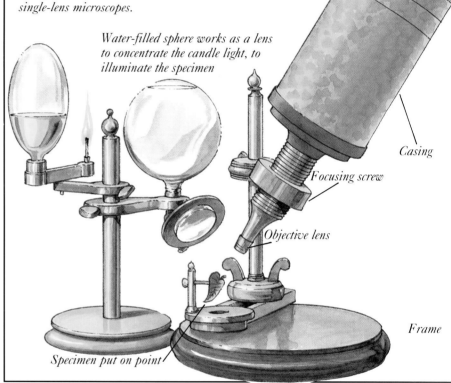

Water-filled sphere works as a lens to concentrate the candle light, to illuminate the specimen

Eyepiece lens

Casing

Focusing screw

Objective lens

Frame

Specimen put on point

DIY SCIENCE

MAKE A MICROSCOPE

You need
Glass tumbler, metal foil, scissors, sticking tape, modelling clay, small mirror, water.

1. Fold the foil as shown to make a thick strip. Punch a small hole in it with the scissors point.

2. Bend the strip and tape it to the tumbler as shown, placing it over the mirror on the clay at 45°.

3. Put the specimen on the tumbler and a small drop of water in the hole, for a lens.

Specimen

Mirror reflects light to illuminate specimen

DIY SCIENCE

People used water-filled bowls as magnifying lenses, for detailed tasks such as sewing and lace-making. This device became known as a lacemaker's condenser.

MAKE A MAGNIFIER

You need
A clear glass or plastic jar with lid, water.

1. Fill the jar with water and screw on the lid. Place it on this book. See how the curved shape works like a lens to magnify the print – but only in one direction. What happens if you turn the jar at right angles?

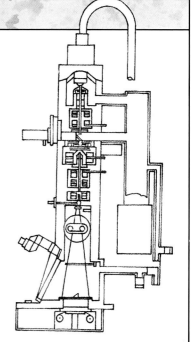

SPECIAL FX

MAKE GIANT SHADOWS!

You need
Torch, object such as fork, spectacle lens with concave shape for short sight.

Shadow

1. Shine the torch on a wall 1 metre away. Place the object so it casts its shadow on the wall. Put the concave lens between them. The lens makes the beam spread out, enlarging the shadow.

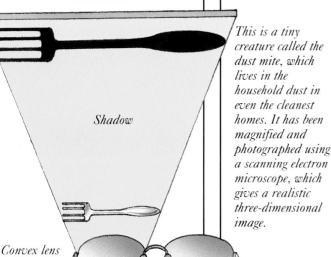

Shadow

Convex lens

FASCINATING FACTS

- There are several types of microscopes. Those using light can magnify up to 1000 or 2000 times. Any bigger, and the view becomes blurred.

- The electron microscope does not use light. It uses beams of atomic particles called electrons. These are focused not by glass lenses, but by magnetic lenses. The electron microscope can magnify objects much more than a light microscope – in some cases, over one million times. This allows the shapes of individual large molecules to be seen.

The electron microscope is a large and expensive device. The electrons are detected and displayed as a visual image on a television screen.

This is a tiny creature called the dust mite, which lives in the household dust in even the cleanest homes. It has been magnified and photographed using a scanning electron microscope, which gives a realistic three-dimensional image.

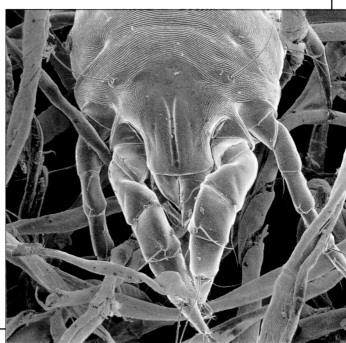

COLOURED LIGHT

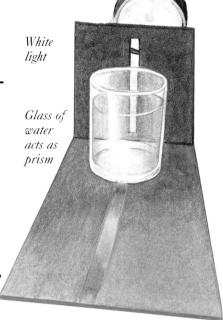

White light

Glass of water acts as prism

White light split into colours

Look around at the colours of things. See how they vary from reds and oranges to yellows, greens, blues and violets – all the colours of the rainbow. They can be bright or dull, vivid or pale. Colours give great pleasure, from beautiful works of art to flowers and birds in nature. Colours also give information, from a red 'stop' light to the green 'all clear'.

Raindrops refract sunlight, splitting it into the colours of the spectrum.

So far in the book, we have seen light being made and detected, and light bouncing and bending. We have used white light and called it 'light' as though it is a single thing. But it is not. White light is a mixture of colours – indeed, all the colours of the rainbow. This extraordinary fact was demonstrated by one of the greatest scientists of all time, Isaac Newton, in about 1665.

In Newton's time, most scientists still believed that white light was a single, pure substance. This idea dated back to the time of Aristotle in Ancient Greece. People had observed that raindrops, lenses, and prisms (blocks of glass with angled sides) seem to turn white light into colours. But they thought that the water droplet or glass added the colours.

Newton showed that white

FAMOUS FIRSTS

NEWTON AND THE PRISM

In 1665, Isaac Newton became interested in light. He experimented using triangle-shaped blocks of glass with angled sides, called prisms. In his day, glass prisms were available as curiosities from travelling fairs. Newton shone a narrow beam of white sunlight through the prism. At a certain angle, the beam which emerged was wider, and it looked like a miniature rainbow – the spectrum. Newton suggested that the different colours which made up white light were being split up because the prism was refracting them by different amounts. This was the opposite view to that of most other scientists, who believed that colours were made by adding something to white light.

Isaac Newton (1642–1727) made tremendous advances in many areas of science, especially in describing the force of gravity and how things move.

The different colours of light are normally hidden by being combined into white light. The angled edge of the glass prism refracts each colour by a slightly different amount and so makes them separate.

DIY SCIENCE

WHITE INTO COLOURS

You can repeat two of Newton's famous experiments. The first shows that white light can be split into colours, but that each colour cannot be split further. The second shows that the various colours obtained by splitting white light, can be combined, back into white light again. You may be able to obtain a prism from a science-supplies shop or a camera and telescope store, or perhaps borrow one (with permission) from a school science laboratory.

You need
Powerful torch with narrow white beam, two prisms, card.

1. In a darkened place, shine the torch beam on to the prism. Move it so the beam reaches the prism's surface at the correct angle, to produce the colours of the spectrum.

2. Shine one colour through a slit in the card, and through a second prism. The beam may spread wider, but is it split into any more colours?

3. For the second experiment, arrange the torch and prism to produce a spectrum, as in step 1.

4. Position the second prism so that it recombines the various colours. The result is white light again.

SPECIAL FX

PRIMARY COLOURS

To make white light, you do not need all the colours of the spectrum. Three are enough – red, green and blue. They are called the primary colours of light, and they combine to make white light. Pigments work in a similar way but give the 'opposite' result. The three primary colours of pigments are yellow, cyan and magenta, and they combine to make black.

The three primary colours of light from three coloured torch beams add up to make whitish light.

The three primary colours of pigments take away all light, so none is reflected, producing the colour black.

FASCINATING FACTS

CHANGING COLOURS

- The colour of an object depends partly on the angle at which light reflects from it. As the sun moves across the sky, the angle of its rays change, and so do the precise colours and hues of things.

Uluru (Ayer's Rock) in Australia, at dawn

The same giant rock at dusk

light was really a mixture or combination of light of different colours. We call them the spectrum, or 'colours of the rainbow'. They are commonly thought of as seven: red, orange, yellow, green, blue, indigo and violet. But if you look carefully at a real spectrum, or the pictures of spectra in this book, you see that the colours are not separate and distinct. They change gradually. One merges into the next. The spectrum is continuous, like a smooth slope, rather than steps of distinct colours.

After Newton's discovery, scientists continued to study colour, both in light, and in the colouring substances we call pigments. Paints contain concentrated pigments, that change the colour of whatever they are painted on. Gradually scientists worked out the relationship between colour, light and pigments. This explains why roses are red, and violets are blue, as follows.

Only certain objects, like the sun or a light bulb, give out light. Most of our familiar light sources make a white or yellowish light. It is this colour because it contains a combination of all the other colours. For other objects, we are able to see them because they reflect light. The colour of an object is due to the colour of light that it reflects. In turn, this depends on the types of pigments that the object contains.

Pigments do not make or create colours. Only things which emit light, from a pocket torch to the sun, can create or generate coloured light. Pigments take in or absorb colours. For example, imagine that white light falls on a tomato. The white light contains all the colours of the spectrum. The pigments in the skin

FAMOUS FIRSTS

THE DYE INDUSTRY

For centuries, people used paints and dyes made from the natural pigments in flowers, minerals and animals. In 1856 William Perkin tried to make drugs from natural tar. Instead he obtained a shining, mauve-purple substance, mauveine. It was one of the first artificial dyes. Today dyeing is a vast industry, producing coloured textiles and materials, from T-shirts to huge carpets.

William Perkin (1838–1907), English chemist

Yellow dye is made from the extract of plants such as dyers' weld or broom.

Ultramarine blue comes from a natural precious stone called lapis lazuli.

Black comes from the soot or carbon left by burning oils, such as linseed oil.

Red comes from the chemical cinnabar, or from plants such as basil or palms.

SPECIAL FX

SEPARATING PIGMENTS

The inks in pens, especially the dark colours, are usually made by combining several different pigments. You can separate these by a process called chromatography.

You need

Tray of water, blotting-paper, string, paper clips, coloured pens with water-soluble inks.

1. Draw a different coloured spot at the base of each strip of blotting paper. Hang the strips as shown, their bases dipping in the water. The water soaks up the strip, carrying the particles of each pigment. The pigments separate according to particle size.

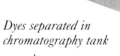

Dyes separated in chromatography tank

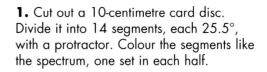

DIY SCIENCE

COLOURS BACK TO WHITE

The colour wheel was devised by Isaac Newton to do the reverse of his famous light-splitting experiment. The idea is to add together the colours of the rainbow, to produce white light.

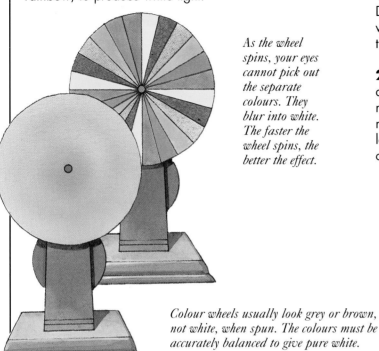

As the wheel spins, your eyes cannot pick out the separate colours. They blur into white. The faster the wheel spins, the better the effect.

Colour wheels usually look grey or brown, not white, when spun. The colours must be accurately balanced to give pure white.

You need
Card, scissors, coloured pens or paints, protractor, pencil.

1. Cut out a 10-centimetre card disc. Divide it into 14 segments, each 25.5°, with a protractor. Colour the segments like the spectrum, one set in each half.

2. Push the pencil though the card's centre and spin it fast, like a top. The colours merge back together to make white, or at least a light-grey or brown.

SPECIAL FX

SEEING INVISIBLE COLOURS

When your eye looks at strong colours for a time, the cells in the sensitive retina which respond to that colour 'get tired'. If you then look away, you may see ghost colours which are opposite, or complementary, to the original colours, as a harmless after-effect.
Stare hard at one of the coloured patterns here for 20 seconds. Then quickly look away at a plain white area. Can you see ghost colours for a few seconds? Draw a chart of each colour's complementary one.

FASCINATING FACTS

- In many countries across the world, green is the colour for 'all clear' or 'go', while red is a colour that represents warnings or danger. Why is this? Could it be that blood is red?

Red is the symbol for 'stop' on traffic lights throughout the world.

of the tomato absorb or take up most of these colours, so that, in effect, they disappear. However the tomato skin's pigments do not absorb the light in the red part of the spectrum. They reflect it. So the only light reflecting off the tomato is the red part of the spectrum. This is the light that reaches your eyes, and you see the tomato as red.

The same happens when light falls on a leaf. But in this case, the colour reflected is green, from the middle of the spectrum. This green light is not used. The light at the red and blue ends of the spectrum is used. It is absorbed by the leaf, and its energy is trapped by the process of photosynthesis (see page 9). If you shone only green light on to a plant, it would still appear green, but it would soon die. The green chemical in plants which takes in the light energy is called chlorophyll. However some plants, such as seaweeds, are not green. They are brown or red. This is because they contain different chemicals for photosynthesis, known as xanthophyll or carotene.

FAMOUS FIRSTS

A BIGGER SPECTRUM

In 1865 James Clerk Maxwell showed that light was one part of a huge range of energy which has the same basic form. This electromagnetic spectrum is made of waves or rays. One wavelength is the distance from a point on one wave, such as the crest or peak, to the same point on the next wave.

Television radio-type waves are only a few metres long.

Radio waves have wavelengths of about a kilometre.

Radar radio-type waves are about 10 centimetres long.

Microwaves have wavelengths of about a centimetre.

Visible light are the only electromagnetic waves that our eyes detect. The other waves are all around us, but we cannot see them.

Infrared waves have wavelengths slightly longer than that of red light.

Ultraviolet waves are shorter than violet light.

James Clerk Maxwell (1831–79) used mathematics to make his discoveries.

Gamma and cosmic rays are incredibly short waves, from space and nuclear reactions which can be dangerous to living things.

X-rays have very short wavelengths. 10 million of them stretch to only one millimetre.

FASCINATING FACTS

• Animals like bees can see ultraviolet rays at one end of the visible spectrum. Others can see infrared rays at the other end. Pit viper snakes have organs under their eyes, which sense the infra-red rays coming from their warm-blooded prey.

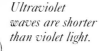

SPECIAL FX

THE COLOUR BOX

You can study the way that light and pigments work using a torch with filters to get rid of certain colours of light, and coloured objects whose surfaces only reflect certain colours of light.

You need

Torch, coloured transparent plastic filters, pieces of fruit, box such as shoe box, scissors, sticky tape.

1. Cut a window in one end of the box to shine the torch through, and a hole in the top to look through. Do the experiments in darkened surroundings. Stick one filter in the window, such as red. Put red, yellow and green apples in the box.

2. Shine the torch in. The red filter removes all colours from the white beam, except red. The red apple reflects this and looks red. The yellow apple reflects some red light and looks duller red. But the green apple has no green light to reflect, and it cannot reflect any other colours. So it appears black.

3. Try other coloured fruits and filters, and see if you can predict the results.

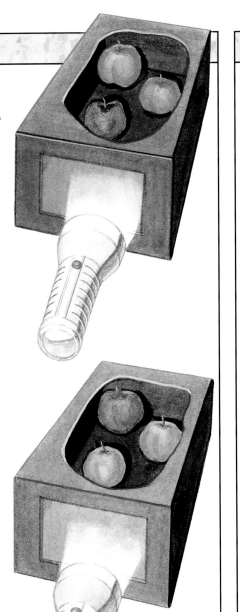

FASCINATING FACTS

A film of soap-and-water produces coloured interference fringes.

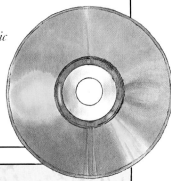

Interference patterns (see below) are responsible for some of the most beautiful colour effects. A thin see-through film, such as a soap bubble or a patch of oil, reflects light from both its surfaces. These are so close that the waves interfere and produce rainbow patterns.

The microscopic pits on a compact disc reflect light in rainbow-like interference colours.

FAMOUS FIRSTS

WHEN LIGHT INTERFERES

English scientist Thomas Young (1773–1829) experimented with interference patterns, which can be explained only if light is in the form of waves, not particles (see page 40). Light passes through small slits close together, and the beams on the other side spread out and overlap as they shine on a screen. If their waves hit the screen in step or in phase, peak to peak, they make a bright patch. If one wave is peaking and the other is a trough, they cancel out and a dark patch results.

Light waves

Bright

If light were particles, these would pass through the slits but not create interference patterns.

Waves of light pass through two narrow, close slits and create dark and light stripes, coloured fringes and other interference patterns.

Dark

MAKING LIGHT WORK

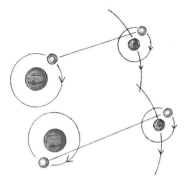

I n our modern world, light is being put to work in an amazing variety of ways. We are trapping sunlight and turning it into electricity and other forms of energy more effectively. And we are using a special form of light, the laser, for all manner of purposes – from repairing diseased eyes, to cutting industrial metals, to reading sounds and images from compact discs.

In the 17th century most scientists believed that light had infinite speed – it took no time at all to travel from one place to another. Further experiments showed that the speed of light is finite, although it is still incredibly fast. Light goes 300,000 kilometres in one second through space, and slower in substances such as glass and water.

It was also believed that light passing through the same substance always travelled in straight lines. But Albert Einstein showed that light can indeed go in a curve under the pull of a star's gravity.

FAMOUS FIRSTS

CURVED LIGHT

Albert Einstein (1879–1955) used mathematics to work out that light bends when it passes near massive objects like stars, due to their immense gravity. He also showed how turning light into electricity, (the photoelectric effect) is explained by light as tiny packets or units, now called photons.

FAMOUS FIRSTS

LIGHT THROUGH NOTHING

Scientists long believed that light could not travel through nothing. It had to go through something. So the idea arose of an invisible substance called ether, which was everywhere – even in space. In 1887 Albert Michelson and Edward Morley used the interference of light (see page 41) to detect ether. They could not, and the idea of ether was disproved.

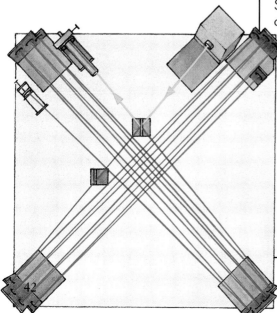

The Michelson–Morley experiment used light beams criss-crossing a huge slab of concrete.

LASER LIGHT

The first laser was made in 1960 by Theodore Maiman. It works by making photons of light strike atoms which have excess energy. These give out more photons, and so on, in a kind of chain reaction. The light from a laser is all the same wavelength, and all waves are in phase (in step). Ordinary light has a mixture of wavelengths and phases.

American scientist Theodore Maiman (1927–) constructed the first working laser, from a ruby crystal that emitted red light.

Laser beams pierce the darkness, and swish across the sky, in spectacular light shows.

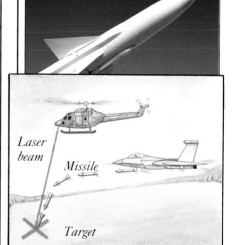

Laser-guided missiles home in on a laser beam shone from an accompanying aircraft, and follow it precisely to the target.

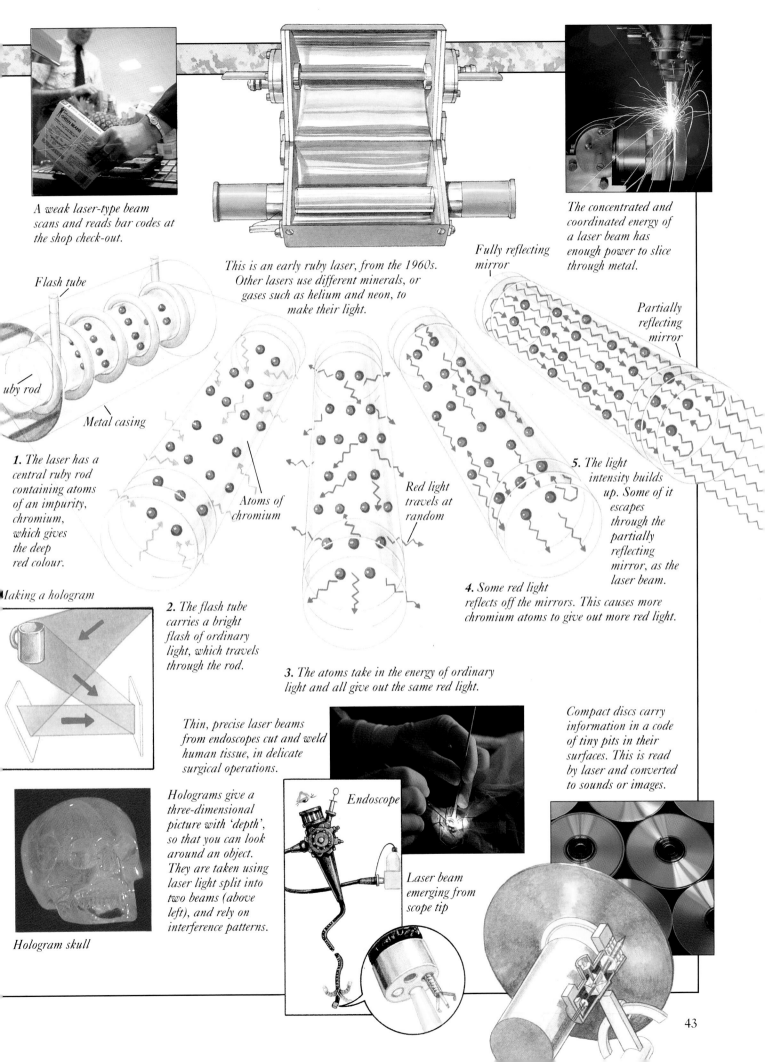

A weak laser-type beam scans and reads bar codes at the shop check-out.

This is an early ruby laser, from the 1960s. Other lasers use different minerals, or gases such as helium and neon, to make their light.

The concentrated and coordinated energy of a laser beam has enough power to slice through metal.

Flash tube

Ruby rod

Metal casing

Fully reflecting mirror

Partially reflecting mirror

1. The laser has a central ruby rod containing atoms of an impurity, chromium, which gives the deep red colour.

Atoms of chromium

Red light travels at random

5. The light intensity builds up. Some of it escapes through the partially reflecting mirror, as the laser beam.

4. Some red light reflects off the mirrors. This causes more chromium atoms to give out more red light.

Making a hologram

2. The flash tube carries a bright flash of ordinary light, which travels through the rod.

3. The atoms take in the energy of ordinary light and all give out the same red light.

Thin, precise laser beams from endoscopes cut and weld human tissue, in delicate surgical operations.

Holograms give a three-dimensional picture with 'depth', so that you can look around an object. They are taken using laser light split into two beams (above left), and rely on interference patterns.

Hologram skull

Endoscope

Laser beam emerging from scope tip

Compact discs carry information in a code of tiny pits in their surfaces. This is read by laser and converted to sounds or images.

43

Newton supported the idea that light energy is in the form of tiny particles or packets called photons. In the 19th century, the idea of light as waves became more popular. Today, we can view light as being particles or waves, depending on which is more convenient. This double-view is called the 'wave-particle duality' of light.

In the 1960s, the science of light entered a new era with the invention of the laser now used in surgery, telecommunications and household goods. Researchers are also working to develop better photovoltaic cells (see page 23), which can produce useful amounts of electricity in the low light levels of overcast conditions, as well as in bright sunlight. If they succeed, these light-powered devices would capture the 'free energy' in sunlight, and contribute greatly to solving the world's energy crisis.

FASCINATING FACTS

- Scientists aimed a laser beam at the moon. It reflected back off a mirror placed there by a space craft. The complete journey took less than three seconds. The returning beam was still as thin as a pencil.

A home fitted with solar panels, to help supply electricity on sunny days.

Solar factories need very large areas to collect enough light.

- Solar cells are becoming more cost-effective. But many people say they are spoiling the landscape.

FAMOUS FIRSTS

LIGHT TO STEER BY
Even in these days of radio-tracking and radar, lighthouses provide a valuable service to ships. Their flashing beacons warn of danger, such as sandbanks just below the surface, or rocky outcrops. The first famous lighthouse was the Pharos Lighthouse of Alexandria, Egypt. It was the sixth of the Seven Ancient Wonders of the World. It was built in 280 BC, but destroyed by earthquake in the 13th century.

A fire of wood or oil burned at the top of the Pharos Lighthouse, 122 metres high. Reflected in polished metal mirrors, it was visible for up to 50 kilometres.

The typical modern lighthouse has a very powerful electric lamp. This stays lit, while lenses rotate around it to make the beam sweep in a circle, and appear to 'flash'.

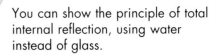

DIY SCIENCE

TALKING WITH LIGHT
When light goes from glass to air, it may be bent by refraction (see page 30). But if it hits the surface at a shallower angle, the light reflects back into the glass, as if from a mirror. This is called total internal reflection. It is the principle behind fibre-optic (optical fibre) communications, where sounds or any other type of information is coded as pulses of laser light.

Laser light travels along the fibre even if it is bent, by reflecting repeatedly in short, straight lines.

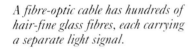

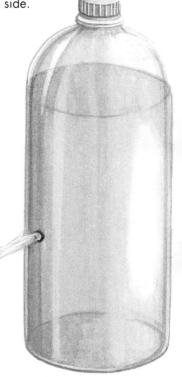

You can show the principle of total internal reflection, using water instead of glass.

You need
Large plastic bottle, water, scissors, powerful torch, darkened conditions.

1. Carefully pierce a small hole in the side of the bottle. Put the bottle in a sink or tray, in a dark place. Fill it with water and shine a torch from the side.

2. The water spurts from the bottle. Adjust the angle of the torch. Its light should carry along the stream of water by total internal reflection, like laser light along an optical fibre. Put your finger in the water to see the beam.

A fibre-optic cable has hundreds of hair-fine glass fibres, each carrying a separate light signal.

Between them, the optical fibres transmit a whole scene, like the inside of these cupped hands.

FASCINATING FACTS

Fibre-optic cables were laid across the Atlantic in 1989 and the Pacific the year after.

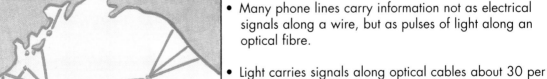

- Many phone lines carry information not as electrical signals along a wire, but as pulses of light along an optical fibre.

- Light carries signals along optical cables about 30 per cent faster than electricity carries signals along metal wires.

- As you talk on the phone, the sounds of your voice are changed to electricity, and then to codes of laser light pulses flashing at over 45 million times each second.

Fibre-optic cables are light and flexible, compared to metal electrical cables.

INDEX